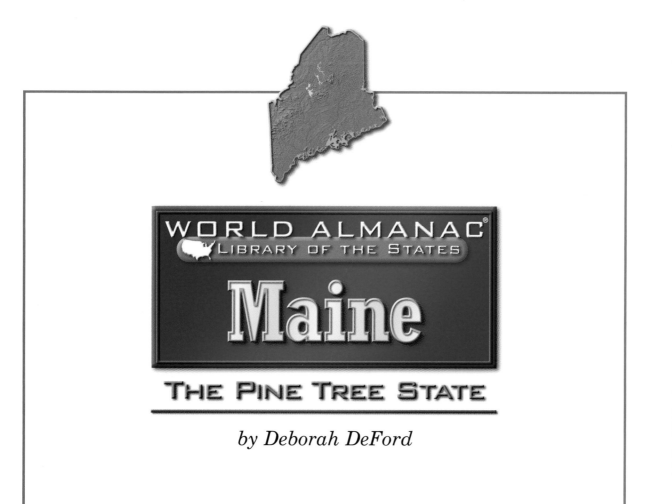

WORLD ALMANAC®
LIBRARY OF THE STATES

Maine

THE PINE TREE STATE

by Deborah DeFord

WORLD ALMANAC® LIBRARY

Please visit our web site at: www.worldalmanaclibrary.com
For a free color catalog describing World Almanac® Library's list of high-quality books
and multimedia programs, call 1-800-848-2928 (USA) or 1-800-387-3178 (Canada).
World Almanac® Library's fax: (414) 332-3567.

Library of Congress Cataloging-in-Publication Data

DeFord, Deborah H.
    Maine, the Pine Tree State / by Deborah DeFord.
       p. cm. — (World Almanac Library of the states)
    Includes bibliographical references and index.
    Summary: Presents the history, geography, people, government, economy,
social life and customs, and state events and attractions of Maine.
    ISBN 0-8368-5151-X (lib. bdg.)
    ISBN 0-8368-5322-9 (softcover)
    1. Maine—Juvenile literature. [1. Maine.] I. Title. II. Series.
F19.3.D44   2003
974.1—dc21
                              2002038096

First published in 2003 by
World Almanac® Library
330 West Olive Street, Suite 100
Milwaukee, WI 53212 USA

Copyright © 2003 by World Almanac® Library.

A Creative Media Applications Production
Design: Alan Barnett, Inc.
Copy editor: Laurie Lieb
Fact checker: Joan Verniero
Photo researcher: Annette Cyr
World Almanac® Library project editor: Tim Paulson
World Almanac® Library editors: Mary Dykstra, Gustav Gedatus, Jacqueline Laks Gorman,
  Lyman Lyons, Jim Mezzanotte
World Almanac® Library art direction: Tammy Gruenewald
World Almanac® Library graphic designers: Scott M. Krall, Melissa Valuch

Photo credits: pp. 4-5 © William Manning/CORBIS; p. 6 (all) © ArtToday; p. 7 (top) © Maine
Office of Tourism; p. 7 (bottom) © Getty Images; p. 9 © North Wind Picture Archives; p. 10
© North Wind Picture Archives; p. 11 © North Wind Picture Archives; p. 12 © Hulton
Archive/Getty Images; p. 13 © Bettmann/CORBIS; p. 14 © AP Photo/The Times Record, Terry
Taylor; p. 15 Courtesy Margaret Chase Smith Library, Skowhegan, ME; p. 17 Courtesy of the
Abbe Museum; p. 18 © Kevin Fleming/CORBIS; p. 19 © Kevin Fleming/CORBIS; p. 20 (left)
© North Wind Picture Archives; p. 20 (center) © Maine Office of Tourism; p. 20 (right)
© N. Carter/North Wind Picture Archives; p. 21 (left) © North Wind Picture Archives; p. 21
(center) © Maine Office of Tourism; p. 21 (right) © Maine Office of Tourism; p. 23 © Maine
Office of Tourism; p. 26 © Maine Office of Tourism; p. 27 © Kevin Fleming/CORBIS; p. 29 © North
Wind Picture Archives; p. 31 (top) © George Bush Presidential Library and Museum; p. 31
(bottom) © Kevin Fleming/CORBIS; p. 32 © Maine Office of Tourism; p. 33 © Maine Office of
Tourism; p. 34 © Maine Office of Tourism; p. 35 © North Wind Picture Archives; p. 36 © John-
Marshall Mantel/CORBIS; p. 37 (top) © AP/Wide World Photos; p. 37 (bottom) © AP/Wide World
Photos; p. 38 © North Wind Picture Archives; p. 39 (left) © North Wind Picture Archives; p. 40
© Bettmann/CORBIS; p. 41 © North Wind Picture Archives; pp. 42-43 © North Wind Picture
Archives; p. 44 © Maine Office of Tourism; p. 45 (top) © Maine Office of Tourism; p. 45 (bottom)
© Maine Office of Tourism

Printed in the United States of America

2 3 4 5 6 7 8 9 07 06 05 04 03

Maine

Rugged Beauty

Maine is a state of dramatic geographic contrasts. Westward from its jagged coast on the Atlantic Ocean, its landscape includes rocky farmlands, vast pine forests, swift-moving rivers, and some of the highest mountains in New England. Small wonder that people from "Down East" take such pride in their state.

The largest of New England's six states, Maine forms the northeastern corner of the United States. The region that is now Maine was home to some of North America's early Native populations, and, later, host to the earliest European explorers and settlers. Despite harsh winters and rough terrain, the region offered an abundance of natural resources that encouraged hearty souls to make it home.

During colonial times, settlers established strong communities in the region, which, at the time, was considered part of the Massachusetts colony. After the Revolutionary War, the settlers pressed for separate state status, which they achieved in 1820. Once Maine established its own state government, its economy blossomed. Water power from rivers aided the growth of factories, while commerce in lumber, shipbuilding, fishing, and granite mining grew.

The state's growing industries brought new waves of inhabitants, and their diversity of talents and ideals produced leaders in government, the military, the arts, and sports. Mainers had strong anti-slavery sentiments, and many of them fought in the Civil War. Later, in the twentieth century, the state sent many soldiers to fight in world wars overseas.

Today, Maine's rugged diversity attracts thousands of visitors every year. It's not surprising that the state is nicknamed "Vacationland." While Mainers welcome tourism and the business it creates, they have never lost the Down East spirit the region and its challenges have bred into them. That spirit remains uniquely their own.

▶ Map of Maine showing the interstate highway system, as well as major cities and waterways.

▼ Every fall, bright, multicolored leaves attract thousands of visitors to Maine.

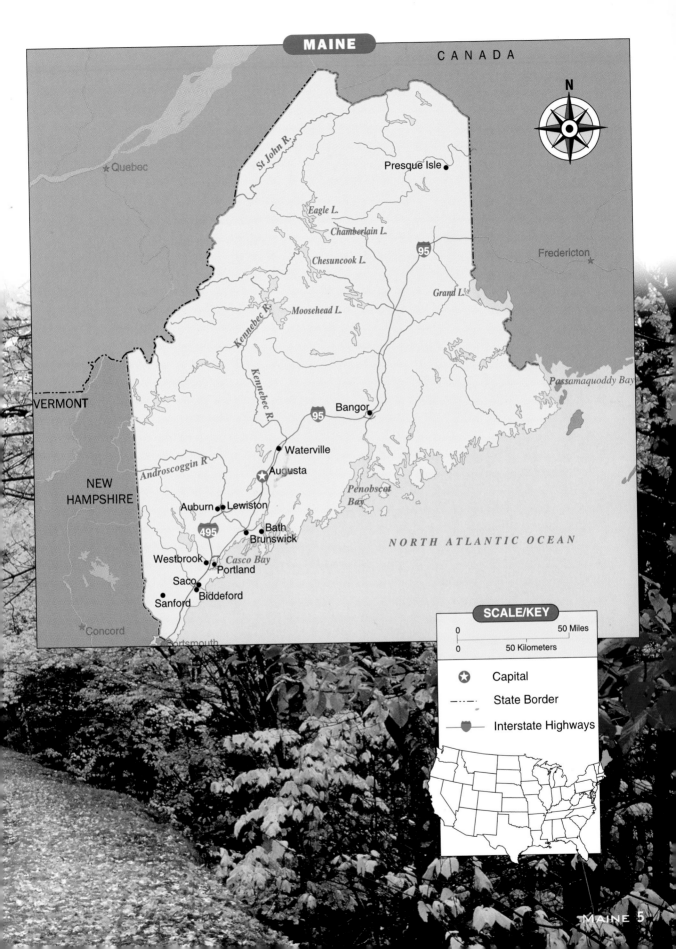

CANADA

★ Quebec

Fredericton

St John R.

Presque Isle ●

Eagle L.

Chamberlain L.

95

Chesuncook L.

Grand L.

Moosehead L.

Kennebec R.

Passamaquoddy Bay

VERMONT

Kennebec R.

95   Bangor ●

NEW
HAMPSHIRE

Androscoggin R.

● Waterville

★ Augusta

Penobscot
Bay

Auburn ● ● Lewiston

NORTH ATLANTIC OCEAN

495

● Bath
Brunswick

Westbrook ●
● Portland

Casco Bay

Saco ●
Sanford ●   ● Biddeford

★ Concord

Portsmouth

SCALE/KEY

0   50 Miles

0   50 Kilometers

★ Capital

State Border

Interstate Highways

Fast Facts

MAINE (ME), The Pine Tree State, Vacationland, Down East

Entered Union

March 15, 1820 (23rd state)

Capital	Population
Augusta	18,560

Total Population (2000)

1,274,923 (40th most populous state) — *Between 1990 and 2000, the state's population increased 3.8 percent.*

Largest Cities	Population
Portland	64,249
Lewiston	35,690
Bangor	31,473
South Portland	23,324
Auburn	23,203

Land Area

30,862 square miles (79,933 square kilometers) (39th largest state)

State Motto

Dirigo — *Latin for* "I direct" *or* "I lead"

State Song

"State of Maine Song," *words and music by Roger Vinton Snow, adopted in 1937.*

State Animal

Moose

State Bird

Chickadee

State Fish

Landlocked salmon

State Cat

Maine coon cat

State Insect

Honeybee

State Flower

White pine cone and tassel

State Tree

White pine

State Mineral

Tourmaline

State Herb

Wintergreen

State Soil

Chesuncook Soil Series

State Fossil

Pertica quadrifaria — *This primitive plant lived 390 million years ago.*

Acadia National Park, *Bar Harbor*
Acadia National Park, the only national park in New England, is located on Mount Desert Island in southeast Maine. The park, with its rocky cliffs and wonderful views of the ocean, occupies more than 47,000 acres (19,000 hectares) of land.

Old Gaol Museum, *York*
This museum is the oldest public building in Maine. Originally used as a "gaol," or jail, it now holds local history relics.

Portland Head Light, *near Portland*
One of the oldest lighthouses in the United States, Portland Head Light was first illuminated in 1791. Its tower is 80 feet (24 meters) high. Today, the lightkeeper's house is a maritime museum.

For other places and events, see p. 44.

BIGGEST, BEST, AND MOST

- Maine's Mt. Katahdin, rising 5,267 feet (1,605 m) above sea level, is the most northern end point of the Appalachian Trail, which begins in Georgia.

- Maine produces more wooden toothpicks (made from white birch) than any other state.

- Rockland has the world's largest lobster boiler. It is 24 feet (7.7 m) long and can steam 5,000 pounds (2,270 kilograms) of lobster in an hour.

STATE FIRSTS

- **1802** Bowdoin College, one of the first colleges in the country to admit African-American students, opened in Brunswick.

- **1851** Maine was the first state to outlaw the sale of alcohol.

- **1922** Maine resident Edwin Arlington Robinson was the first poet to win a Pulitzer Prize.

- **1948** Margaret Chase Smith of Maine became the first woman ever to be voted into a full term in the U.S. Senate.

Lobsters Galore

People often think of tasty lobsters when they think of Maine — and for good reason! Maine has the nation's largest lobster catch, which totals about 50 million pounds (23 million kg) per year. Lobster shacks are standard fare in every harbor, and lobster boats dot the shoreline waters. Special cages, called pots, are dropped to the bottom of the sea near the shore where these crustaceans live and feed. When female lobsters are caught they are thrown back, so they can lay eggs that produce more lobsters. The average Maine lobster weighs about 1.5 pounds (0.7 kg), but a Maine lobster can weigh up to 20 pounds (9 kg).

Earmuff Capital

Next time you put on a pair of earmuffs to keep your ears warm, remember Maine! The town of Farmington was once called the "Earmuff Capital of the World." In 1873, a fifteen-year-old boy named Chester Greenwood, who lived in Farmington, invented the first pair of earmuffs. He went on to patent his invention on March 13, 1877. Greenwood then built a factory where earmuffs were mass-produced. His warm, practical ear coverings were a huge success. Every winter, Farmington honors its most famous citizen with an annual Chester Greenwood Day.

The Past of the Pine Tree State

> In order to promote the interests and encourage the industry of all the inhabitants of the countries watered by the river St. John and its tributaries . . . it is agreed that . . . the river St. John is declared to be the line of boundary . . . That all the produce of the forest . . . grown on any of those parts of the State of Maine watered by the river St. John . . . shall have free access into and through the said river . . . having their source within the State of Maine.
>
> — *The Webster-Ashburton Treaty, 1842*

During the Ice Age, about two million years ago, huge sheets of moving ice, called glaciers, covered what is now Maine. As temperatures rose, the glaciers receded, creating much of Maine's present landscape. The first people to live in the region probably arrived about ten thousand years ago, and some of the area's oldest artifacts date back three thousand years. Later, peoples that were part of the Algonquian group of Native Americans, including the Abenaki and Etchemin (who gave rise to the Maliseet and Passamaquoddy), lived in the region. They built villages but often moved from place to place, hunting and gathering their food. More warlike tribes, such as the Micmac, also roamed the land, hunting and fishing to survive.

Exploration and Settlement

By comparison, Europeans were latecomers to the region. Many scholars believe that John Cabot, an Italian explorer sent by England, may have been the first European to set foot in Maine, in 1498. In 1524, Giovanni da Verrazano arrived from France. Verrazano did not stay long, but more European explorers followed. French explorer Samuel de Champlain traveled the St. Croix River and named Mount Desert Island, Maine's largest seacoast island.

In the early seventeenth century, Europeans began settling in the region. After hearing favorable reports

Native Americans of Maine

Abenaki

Etchemin

Maliseet

Micmac

Passamaquoddy

Penobscot

DID YOU KNOW?

No one knows for sure how Maine got its name. Some believe it comes from English explorers who used the term "the mainland" to refer to land on shore rather than islands. Others believe it comes from the French word *Maine*, an ancient province of France.

about the region, Ferdinando Gorges and John Popham of England sent George Waymouth to explore the coast and establish a colony of settlers. The colony, called the Popham Plantation, was founded in 1607 near the Kennebec River, but it lasted only one year. The settlers gave up the colony after trouble with the region's Native peoples and the death of their leader, George Popham.

Over the next twenty years, both English and French colonists claimed land in the region. In 1622, the British government gave Gorges and George Mason a large tract of land in present-day Maine and New Hampshire. The two men divided the land in 1629, with Gorges taking the Maine region. Gorges established the region's first government in 1636. Coastal communities developed in the region, as settlers cut trees from its dense forests, fished its waters, farmed its rocky soil, and braved its harsh winters.

Gorges died in 1647. In 1658, the region came under the control of the Massachussetts Bay Colony. Gorges's family challenged this arrangement, however, and the British government gave the region back to the family. Then, in 1677, the Massachusetts Bay Colony regained control of Maine when it bought the region from the Gorges family.

▼ Throughout Maine, Algonquian people built villages and lived in dome-shaped houses.

MAINE

French and Indian War

The ongoing struggle between England and France for control of the colonies led to a series of battles between 1689 and 1763. In Maine and elsewhere, Native Americans often sided with the French, because the French traded with the Native Americans while the English continued to claim Native American lands. The trouble eventually led, in 1754, to the French and Indian War, which continued until 1763. In Maine, the French encouraged the Native peoples to attack villages in hopes of driving out British settlers.

The war finally ended with French defeat and the signing of the Treaty of Paris, which gave the British control of most of North America. A large number of Native peoples fled to Canada, leaving Maine's Native population significantly smaller.

The Revolutionary War

By the 1760s, the people of Maine had joined other colonists in a growing dislike of British rule. The French and Indian War had cost the British dearly, and to help pay the war's expense, they passed laws that taxed the colonists and restricted their trade. In 1774, a group of Maine colonists

◀ This woodcut from Benjamin Lossing's book *Our Country* (1905) shows a group of colonial soldiers crossing the mountains during the French and Indian War. The soldiers' travels led some of them later to move their families from Maine's coast to its interior.

in York responded by burning English tea, a taxed item. The York Tea Party was Maine's version of the more famous Boston Tea Party, which took place in 1773.

When the Revolutionary War began in 1775, the people of Maine were sandwiched between the strongly patriotic New England colonies and the mostly loyalist colonists in Canada. Maine's extensive coastline could easily be attacked and taken. The colonists knew they needed a strong defense in order to survive.

In June 1775, the Maine militia captured the British ship *Margaretta* off the coast near the town of Machias — the first naval battle of the Revolutionary War. The British retaliated by firing red-hot cannonballs into Falmouth (now Portland), burning down most of the city. About six thousand Maine colonists fought in the American Revolution, resulting in about one thousand deaths.

After the war, in 1783, Massachusetts rewarded its soldiers by selling Maine land to them for less than a dollar an acre. The reward drew so many people from Massachusetts and New Hampshire that Maine's population swelled from 56,000 in 1784 to 96,540 in 1791.

Maine Becomes a State

In 1785, some Maine residents began arguing for separation from Massachusetts. The government of Massachusetts, they argued, taxed them too heavily and gave too little in return. They also believed Mainers were too far from the seat of government, in Boston, to influence what laws were passed. At the time, however, the majority of the people in Maine favored staying part of Massachusetts.

Sentiment changed in 1812, when the United States once again went to war against Great Britain. During the conflict, British troops raided the Maine coast and significantly damaged its shipping industry. Clearly, Massachusetts either could not or would not adequately protect Maine.

Hannibal Hamlin

Hannibal Hamlin, born in 1809 in Paris Hill, became one of the nation's great lawmakers. He served in the U.S. House of Representatives from 1843 to 1847 and in the U.S. Senate from 1848 to 1856. In 1857, he was elected Maine's governor, but he returned to the U.S. Senate later that year. Hamlin opposed slavery, a view strongly shared by many Mainers of the time. In the 1850s, Hamlin helped form the anti-slavery political organization that became the Republican Party. When Abraham Lincoln ran for U.S. president as a Republican in 1860 — a race he won — he chose Hamlin as his vice presidential candidate. As the Civil War raged during Lincoln's first term, Hamlin fought for the end of legal slavery in both northern and southern states. Later in his political career, he returned to the U.S. Senate to battle for equal rights for African Americans in the South. He went on to serve as minister to Spain from 1881 to 1882. Hamlin died in 1891.

Statehood now looked like the best choice for Maine, even to merchants who benefited from Massachusetts rule.

In a referendum in 1819, the vast majority of Maine inhabitants voted to separate from Massachusetts. On March 15, 1820, Maine became a state, with William King its first governor and the city of Portland its first capital. (Augusta became the capital in 1832.)

Maine's admittance as a state played an important role in the Missouri Compromise. At the time, the anti-slavery North and pro-slavery South typically allowed new states to enter the Union in pairs — one a "slave state," where slavery was legal, and one a "free state," where slavery was illegal. Northern leaders wanted all new states west of the Mississippi River to be free states. Southern leaders disagreed. A heated debate arose when Missouri (west of the Mississippi) sought slave-state status in 1819. The Missouri Compromise allowed Missouri to enter the Union as a slave state and Maine to enter as a free state, keeping the balance intact.

A decade later, Maine once more found itself at the heart of controversy. A long-standing dispute over the border between Canada and Maine led to the Aroostook War of 1839, in which militias were called up but no fighting took

▼ In this Currier & Ives print, General Winfield Scott Hancock leads the Union charge on Confederate troops during the Battle of Spotsylvania in Virginia during the Civil War.

place. Instead, General Winfield Scott, representing the United States, met with members of the Canadian government to work out a temporary agreement. It was followed by the Webster-Ashburton Treaty of 1842, which finally set Maine's boundary with Canada.

Growth in the 1800s

Maine continued to grow during the 1800s. It sold large quantities of lumber to other states, and Bath became the nation's leading city for shipbuilding. Potatoes, which grew well in much of Maine, became the primary crop by the 1820s. By midcentury, cloth and leather factories also were established. In the late 1800s, towns such as Westbrook, Yarmouth, and Mechanic Falls had thriving paper mills.

The Civil War and After

During Maine's period of economic growth, the state's anti-slavery sentiments grew as well. Brunswick resident Harriet Beecher Stowe wrote *Uncle Tom's Cabin* (1852). The book was widely read, and it added energy to the efforts of people working to end slavery — one of the issues that fueled the Civil War (1861–1865), the bloody conflict between the anti-slavery (Union) North and the pro-slavery (Confederate) South.

Anti-slavery Maine played its part in the war. Its former governor and lawmaker, Hannibal Hamlin, served as vice president under U.S. president Abraham Lincoln for the war's duration. Two of the Union's great generals, Oliver Otis Howard and Joshua L. Chamberlain, came from Maine. More than seventy thousand Mainers fought in the Union army, and about seventy-five hundred of them were killed. When the North won, slavery became illegal.

While the human effects of the war were terrible, its economic effects for Maine were mostly positive. The state's textile and leather industries grew as they supplied the Union army. As people migrated to the cities to work in the factories, however, rural communities shrank.

Maine continued to grow in the years following the Civil War. The first railroads arrived during the late 1800s. The most important of these was the Aroostook Railroad, which took potatoes from Aroostook County to market. The

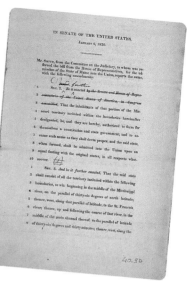

▲ This Senate bill, dated January 6, 1820, admits Maine to the Union and authorizes the creation of Missouri, a slave state.

Flags and Pride

Maine's state flag is based on one used by its troops until the time of the Civil War. A blue flag showing Maine's coat of arms, it became the state flag in 1909. When Maine gained statehood in 1820, legislators added the North Star to the flag, signifying Maine's status as the nation's northern-most state. The North Star is a navigational guide for sailors, so the symbol also has meaning for the many seafaring people of Maine.

textile and paper industries grew, with more trees cut for paper products than for lumber. The invention of the steamship helped transform the state's shipbuilding industry. Demand for wooden sailing ships dropped, but the Bath Iron Works was established, and the state began producing steel ships.

Wars and Hard Times

When the Spanish-American War erupted in 1898, Mainers were once again part of U.S. troops. They also fought in World War I, which began in Europe in 1914 but did not involve the United States until 1917. Maine contributed steel ships and about thirty-five thousand soldiers to the war effort.

In the early 1900s, the state built dams to harness water power, greatly increasing its electricity production, and in 1929 the sale of hydroelectricity outside the state was forbidden by popular vote. From 1929 to 1939, Maine suffered with the rest of the nation through the hard economic times of the Great Depression. As was happening across the land, businesses, farms, and banks failed. World War II (1939–1945) helped bring about the end of the Depression. In Maine, the economy strengthened as U.S. armed forces commissioned hundreds of submarines and ships for the war, as well as soldiers' boots and uniforms. Ninety-five thousand Mainers, both women and men, served in World War II, with two thousand casualties.

Postwar to Present

Since World War II, Maine has had its economic ups and downs. The state became a summer and winter vacation destination after the war, when a new generation of tourists discovered the beauty of Maine's coastline, islands, forests, and mountains. The 1950s and 1960s saw the growth of electronics companies and food-packaging factories, as well as the establishment of U.S. Air Force bases, but in the 1970s, 1980s, and 1990s, the fishing and paper industries

▲ Maine made an important contribution to the Allied victory in World War II with ships and other wartime machinery built at the Bath Iron Works, shown above. This shipbuilding facility continues to be an important part of Maine's economy today.

DID YOU KNOW?

Maine has always been one of the nation's most productive shipbuilding centers. By 1900, 50 percent of all U.S. ships came from Maine. Many of the ships were built at Maine's major shipyard — the Bath Iron Works.

shrank. Tourism and other service industries increased, however, and today, economic growth in Maine continues. Specialized farming supplies foods to much of the Northeast, while new industries regularly move into the state. In addition, the state's tourist industry continues to expand.

Maine's Native Americans, whose lands were improperly seized from them in the colonial era, never shared in the state's economic growth. Native American tribes in Maine filed a lawsuit to recover damages, however, and, in 1980, the U.S. government accepted their claim, paying the Maliseet, Passamaquoddy, and Penobscot $81.5 million. These Native American groups invested their money in forest lands and blueberry fields.

The economy of Maine depends heavily on its natural resources, so conserving those assets continues to rank high as a concern among the state's residents. Besides working to pass laws that preserve the environment, Maine's legislators have addressed the overharvesting of timber, pollution of waterways, effects of forest fires, and commercial development of wilderness areas.

Margaret Chase Smith

Born in Skowhegan in 1897, Margaret Chase Smith began work as a teacher. In 1940, however, when her husband died in office, she served out the rest of his term in the U.S. House of Representatives. She won reelection to four more terms. In 1948, she became the first woman elected to a full term in the U.S. Senate and the first woman to serve in both houses. Smith also waged a campaign to win the Republican presidential nomination in the 1964 election — another first for U.S. women. Smith died at the age of 98 in 1995.

Below: Senator Margaret Chase Smith is greeted enthusiastically at the Republican National Convention in San Francisco in 1964.

Room for Individualists

As Maine goes, so goes the nation.
— *American political maxim, c. 1888*

Maine is not a populous state, especially compared to other states. In the year 2000, its population was 1,274,923, an increase of only 3.8 percent from ten years earlier, and it ranked fortieth out of the fifty states in size of population. The state's population density — the number of people, on average, who live within a square mile of land — is also quite low. Maine's density is 41.3 people per square mile (15.9 per sq km). Compared to New Jersey, the most densely populated state, which has 1,134.5 people per square mile (438.1 per sq km), Maine has a lot of room.

About half of Maine's population live in urban areas clustered along its coast. The city of Portland has the highest population, followed by Lewiston, Bangor, South Portland, and Auburn. Many people in Maine, however,

Age Distribution in Maine (2000 Census)	
0–4	70,726
5–19	264,759
20–24	69,656
25–44	370,597
45–64	315,783
65 & over	183,402

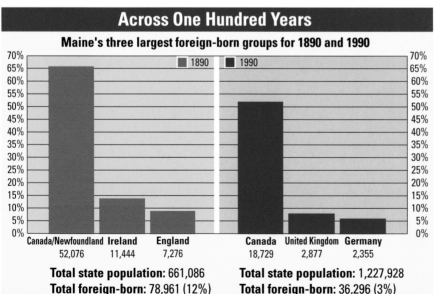

Across One Hundred Years

Maine's three largest foreign-born groups for 1890 and 1990

■ 1890   ■ 1990

Canada/Newfoundland 52,076 — Ireland 11,444 — England 7,276

Canada 18,729 — United Kingdom 2,877 — Germany 2,355

Total state population: 661,086
Total foreign-born: 78,961 (12%)

Total state population: 1,227,928
Total foreign-born: 36,296 (3%)

Patterns of Immigration

The total number of people who immigrated to Maine in 1998 was 709. Of that number, the largest immigrant groups came from Canada (12.2%), China (11.3%), and Russia (8.2%).

enjoy the state's open spaces away from the cities. These areas provide a high quality of life, with less pollution, small, tight-knit communities, and plenty of opportunities for outdoor recreation.

Despite Maine's relatively low population, its residents take an active role in governing the state. Maine often ranks highest among the fifty states in voter turnout. The state also has one of the lowest crime rates in the United States, another factor that contributes to a high quality of life.

Ethnicity

Native Americans were Maine's first inhabitants, but only about seven thousand of their descendants lived in the state in 2000. Four Native American groups — the Penobscot, Passamaquoddy, Maliseet, and Micmac — are officially recognized by the state and the federal government. At various times since 1980, these groups have received federal grants to purchase land.

When European settlement began in Maine, English and French settlers were most prominent. Later, Scotch-Irish and French-Canadian immigrants seeking economic

▲ Reuben Phillips, a Penobscot elder, views a time line of his tribal history at the Abbe Museum in Bar Harbor.

DID YOU KNOW?

Many of the names of Maine's geographical features come from Native American words. *Katahdin*, for example, the name of the state's tallest peak, means "principal mountain."

Heritage and Background, Maine   Year 2000

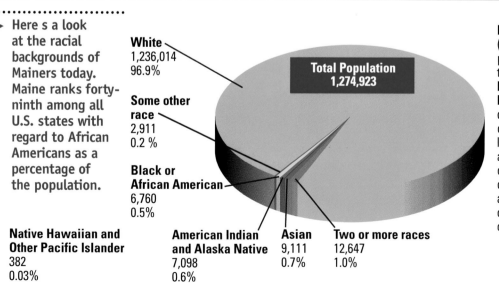

▶ Here s a look at the racial backgrounds of Mainers today. Maine ranks forty-ninth among all U.S. states with regard to African Americans as a percentage of the population.

White
1,236,014
96.9%

Some other race
2,911
0.2 %

Black or African American
6,760
0.5%

Total Population 1,274,923

Note: 0.7% (9,360) of the population identify themselves as **Hispanic** or **Latino,** a cultural designation that crosses racial lines. Hispanics and Latinos are counted in this category as well as the racial category of their choice.

Native Hawaiian and Other Pacific Islander
382
0.03%

American Indian and Alaska Native
7,098
0.6%

Asian
9,111
0.7%

Two or more races
12,647
1.0%

opportunities moved into the state. The term "New England Yankees" commonly refers to people of English and Scotch-Irish descent — people traditionally considered to be fiercely independent, sturdy, and frugal individualists. Stereotypes aside, it took such qualities to survive and thrive in Maine's harsh climate and rugged geography. Today, most Maine residents are of European descent, but the state does have other ethnic groups. As of the 2000 Census, Maine had 9,360 Hispanics, 6,760 African Americans, and 9,111 Asians.

Religion

Most of the first English settlers in Maine were Protestants — strict Puritans from the Massachusetts Bay Colony. Today, Maine's Protestants belong to many denominations

Educational Levels of Maine Workers (age 25 and over)	
Less than 9th grade	47,183
9th to 12th grade, no diploma	80,105
High school graduate, including equivalency	314,600
Some college, no degree or associate degree	229,045
Bachelor's degree	129,992
Graduate or professional degree	68,968

▼ A variety of buildings line the shores of Casco Bay in Portland, Maine's largest city.

and include Baptists, Presbyterians, Congregationalists, and Methodists.

Maine's French-Canadian population is primarily Roman Catholic, numbering about 264,000. The state has a relatively small Jewish population of 8,000.

Another religious group, known as the Shakers, has its last surviving community in the nation near New Gloucester. Founded in the late eighteenth century, the group got its name from the way its members would shake in religious ecstasy during services. Shakers do not marry and own few worldly goods.

▲ Students enjoy a warm day at Bowdoin College in Brunswick. Chartered in 1794, Bowdoin is one of the oldest colleges in Maine.

Education

Maine's population was sparse in colonial days, so ministers and parents often served as a community's only teachers. The first school may have been an Indian mission founded by a Roman Catholic priest in 1696. Not until the early 1700s do records show towns hiring schoolmasters for their children. Maine's first schoolhouse was built in York in 1724. An education law passed in 1789 required towns to assume responsibility for the operation of schools. By 1820, Maine had 236 tax-supported elementary schools and twenty-five academies.

Today, a nine-member board of education and a commissioner of education run Maine's public schools. State law requires children to attend school from the age of seven to seventeen. The state's schools provide excellent math, reading, and science programs, and many students earn high scores on national achievement tests.

The University of Maine, whose main campus is in Orono, is the largest of the state's institutions for higher education, with about 19,700 students. Smaller private colleges include Colby College in Waterville, Bowdoin College in Brunswick, and New England's first coeducational college, Bates College in Lewiston. The state also supports the Maine Maritime Academy in Castine and numerous technical schools for electronics, engineering, and agriculture.

French Acadians of Maine

During the French and Indian War, the British and French fought for possession of land in Maine and Canada. As the British forces moved into Nova Scotia in 1755, they conquered a group of French colonists known as French Acadians. Forced to leave their colony, many of these Acadians moved into northern Maine. Their descendants form one of the largest ethnic groups in Maine today.

Coast, Farmland, and Mountains

> O Pine Tree State,
> Your woods, fields and hills,
> Your lakes, streams and rock bound coast
> Will ever fill our hearts with thrills,
> And tho' we seek far and wide
> Our search will be in vain,
> To find a fairer spot on earth
> Than Maine! Maine! Maine!
>
> — *"State of Maine Song" by Roger Vinton Snow*

Only eleven states in the United States are smaller than Maine. Among the six New England states, however, Maine is the largest, with a total area of 30,862 square miles (79,933 sq km).

Maine can be divided into three geographic regions: the Coastal Lowlands, the Eastern New England Upland, and the White Mountains Region. The three regions have distinct differences in climate, soil, wildlife, and terrain.

The Coastal Lowlands

The Coastal Lowlands consists of the southeastern part of Maine. Stretching along the coast of the state, the area is part of a larger region of the same name that runs along the New England seaboard. From the ocean, the Coastal Lowlands extends westward anywhere from 10 to 40 miles

Highest Point

Mount Katahdin
5,267 feet (1,605 m)
above sea level

▼ *From left to right:* Maine's rocky coast; fields of potato blossoms; wild blueberries; fall foliage; West Quoddy Head Lighthouse; Popham Beach.

(16 to 64 km). Although most of this region now lies at sea level, it once rose much higher. During the Ice Age, the enormous weight of the glaciers' ice and snow depressed the land to its present elevation.

Maine's 228-mile (367-km) coast varies greatly from one end to the other. At the southern end of the coast, beachgoers enjoy long stretches of hard-packed, smooth sand. Toward the north, the beaches become shorter and stonier and are broken up by rocky cliffs. Just inland from the sea, saltwater makes its way through tidal creeks and salt marshes. Deep bays and harbors all along the coast help make sailing and shipping a major part of the state's coastal activity, and thousands of islands dot the coastal waters. Once hilltops, these land masses were stranded when melting glaciers raised the level of the sea. Mount Desert Island, which is Maine's largest island, measures about 100 square miles (259 sq km).

The Eastern New England Upland

The region known as the Eastern New England Upland stretches from Connecticut to the border of Canada. In Maine, it lies just northwest of Maine's Coastal Lowlands, ranging in width from 20 to 50 miles (32 to 80 km). This region varies dramatically in elevation, with some areas at sea level and others as high as 2,000 feet (610 m). In the northeast part of the upland lies a large, flat region with rich, deep soil called the Aroostook Plateau. Here, Maine farmers grow most of the state's potatoes, providing the third largest potato crop in the nation. South of the plateau, there are numerous upland lakes, as well as swift-moving streams fed by springs and, after winter, melting snow. In the central part of the region, a ridge of mountainous terrain rises. This stunningly beautiful terrain includes several important wildlife habitats.

Average January temperature
Caribou: 9°F (-13°C)
Portland: 21°F (-6°C)

Average July temperature
Caribou: 61°F (16°C)
Portland: 62°F (17°C)

Average yearly rainfall
Caribou: 38 inches (97 cm)
Portland: 42 inches (107 cm)

Average yearly snowfall
Caribou: 112 inches (284 cm)
Portland: 72 inches (183 cm)

DID YOU KNOW?

Maine is the only state that borders on only one state — New Hampshire to the west. The Atlantic Ocean and Canada are Maine's other borders.

Largest Lakes

Moosehead Lake
76,800 acres (31,081 ha)

Sebago Lake
28,771 acres (11,644 ha)

Grand Lake
16,070 acres (6,504 ha)

MAINE GEOGRAPHY

N

SCALE/KEY

| 0 | 50 Miles |
| 0 | 50 Kilometers |

NP	National Park
▲	Highest Point
▲	Important Peaks
	Mountains

The White Mountains Region

The White Mountains Region extends from New Hampshire and Vermont into the north-central part of Maine, where the region's mountain range is known as the Longfellow Mountains. This region measures about 5 miles (8 km) wide in the north and up to 30 miles (48 km) wide in the south. The state's highest mountain peaks — including Katahdin, Bigelow, and Saddleback — and hundreds of lakes of all sizes are located in this region.

Plants and Animals

Maine, the Pine Tree State, is covered with more woodland than any other state — about 90 percent of its land area.

White pine, the state tree, is just one of a variety of trees in the state — there are also birch, spruce, balsam fir, beech, hemlock, maple, oak, and basswood. A shrub called speckled alder grows widely in the swamps, and wild blueberry bushes abound, yielding a big crop.

An assortment of beautiful wildflowers grow in Maine. The most common are buttercup, anemone, black-eyed Susan, aster, Indian pipe, and daisy. In wooded areas, delicate lady's slipper can be found. Lavender and lily of the valley grow wild near lakes and on the coast.

Wildlife also flourishes in Maine. More than twenty thousand moose wander wild. The moose is the state animal and often weighs about 1,500 pounds (680 kg). Mountains and forests provide homes for black bears, bobcats, white-tailed deer, foxes, mink, beavers, raccoon, and lynx.

Maine's streams and lakes abound with freshwater fish, including smallmouth bass, pickerel, perch, brook trout, and landlocked salmon. Fish called alewives swim up coastal rivers in spring to lay eggs, then return to the sea. Some rivers contain Atlantic salmon, and coastal waters have flounder, pollock, striped bass, and cod. Out at sea, whales draw many observers each year.

More than 320 types of birds can be found in Maine, including the puffin, which breeds regularly in no other eastern state. Birds such as owls, grackles, chickadees, buntings, and swallows thrive on the mainland. Other birds can be found on the state's coastal islands, including loons, gulls, cormorants, terns, and ducks.

Major Rivers

St. John River
418 miles (673 km)

Penobscot River
350 miles (563 km)

Kennebec River
190 miles (306 km)

Androscoggin River
175 miles (282 km)

St. Croix River
75 miles (121 km)

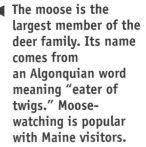

◄ The moose is the largest member of the deer family. Its name comes from an Algonquian word meaning "eater of twigs." Moose-watching is popular with Maine visitors.

Trade and Paper Mills

> Sawing plank was a laborious process . . . The man in the pit faced the direction of the saw cut, to avoid sawdust, and by alternately pulling on the saw, the man could rip a log into a plank. The work was slow and required so much work that the "sawyer" became a recognized trade.
>
> — *A historian of Maine's shipbuilding as quoted in* Down East: A Maritime History of Maine *by Lincoln P. Paine, 2000*

Maine's economy has undergone many changes during its history. At first, Maine's vast forests provided fuel as well as lumber for its thriving shipbuilding industry. Eventually, however, oil and coal became more common fuels than wood, the shipbuilding industry turned away from wooden sailing ships and began producing steamships made of iron and steel, and Maine's forests became more important for supplying a successful paper industry than for providing lumber. During the mid-1800s, Maine was home to a growing textile industry, but this industry declined when textile factories moved to the South, where manufacturing costs were lower. Today, manufacturing continues to be a part of Maine's economy, as does fishing and farming, and the state's natural beauty supports a growing tourist industry. The largest part of the state's economy, however, is now the service industry, and its most valuable economic resource is its people.

Fishing, Agriculture, Forestry, and Mining

Maine's coastal harbors, the largest of which are Portland and Rockland, support numerous small fleets of fishing boats that bring in a wide variety of fish and shellfish. Maine's lobstermen catch more lobsters annually than any group in the nation. Overall, the fishing industry is currently worth about $324 million per year.

Top Employers
(of workers age sixteen and over)

Services	41.9%
Wholesale and retail trade	16.9%
Manufacturing	14.2%
Construction	6.9%
Transportation, communications, and other public utilities	6.8%
Finance, insurance, and real estate	6.2%
Federal, state, and local government (including military)	4.5%
Agriculture, forestry, fisheries, and mining	2.6%

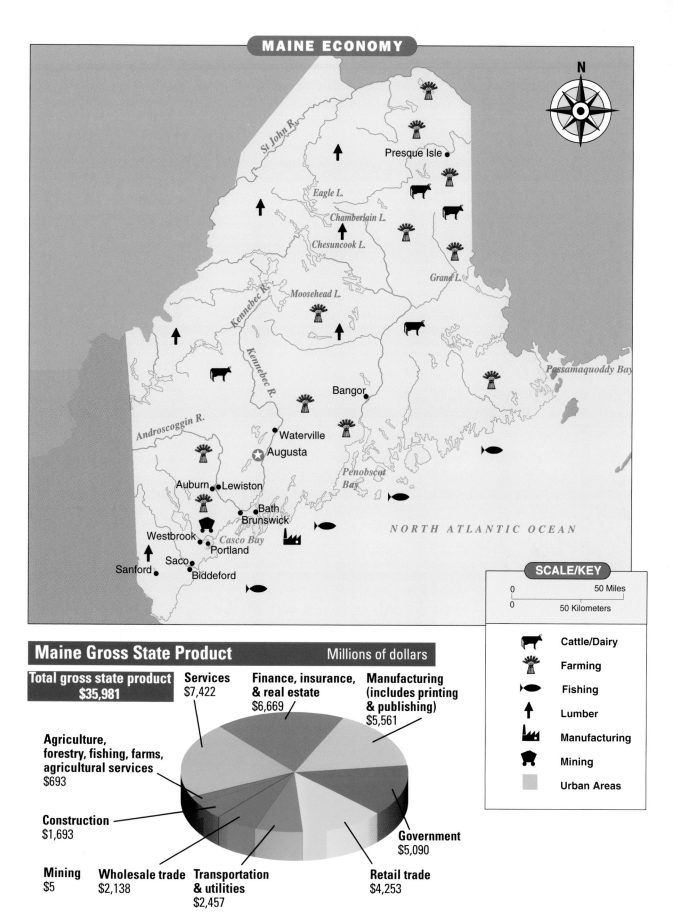

MAINE ECONOMY

St John R.

Presque Isle

Eagle L.

Chamberlain L.

Chesuncook L.

Grand L.

Moosehead L.

Kennebec R.

Passamaquoddy Bay

Kennebec R.

Bangor

Androscoggin R.

Waterville

Augusta

Penobscot Bay

Auburn • Lewiston

Bath

Brunswick

NORTH ATLANTIC OCEAN

Westbrook

Casco Bay

Portland

Sanford • Saco

Biddeford

SCALE/KEY

0	50 Miles
0	50 Kilometers

Cattle/Dairy

Farming

Fishing

Lumber

Manufacturing

Mining

Urban Areas

Maine Gross State Product — Millions of dollars

Total gross state product $35,981

Services $7,422

Finance, insurance, & real estate $6,669

Manufacturing (includes printing & publishing) $5,561

Agriculture, forestry, fishing, farms, agricultural services $693

Construction $1,693

Mining $5

Wholesale trade $2,138

Transportation & utilities $2,457

Retail trade $4,253

Government $5,090

Agriculture is also an important part of the economy. About seventy-four hundred farms produce the state's primary crops — blueberries, potatoes, oats, hay, apples, and corn. Maine leads the nation in blueberry production and is the third-largest potato producer. Some farms also raise turkeys, sheep, chickens, pigs, and dairy herds. Eggs and milk are the most significant livestock products.

Maine's forests are a huge natural resource — over 90 percent of its land area is covered in forest, more than any other state — and this resource continues to be a big part of the state's economy. It generates jobs in the logging industry and in paper and pulp mills.

Mining makes up a very small part (.01 percent) of the state's economy. The most important materials mined include the gemstone tourmaline, slate deposits, sand and gravel, garnet, and peat. Although southern Maine contains many limestone and granite deposits, they are not mined.

Manufacturing

Manufacturing makes up about 15 percent of Maine's gross state product (GSP) — the total value of goods and services produced in the state in a year. Of the manufactured goods in the state, paper goods, such as pulp, paper, cardboard boxes, and paper bags, bring in the greatest revenue. Fir and spruce trees are used to make most of these products. The paper industry is a major employer for Maine, with pulp and paper mills found in many cities in the state.

Wood products are next in significance in Maine. The most important is lumber, and northern Maine is home to many lumber camps and sawmills. The state's wood is also used to make toothpicks, and in fact the state is the nation's leading toothpick producer. Other paper products include lobster traps, clothespins, and matches.

Next in prominence among manufactured goods is transportation equipment, including ships and boats.

▲ Farm workers pick blueberries in a Maine field.

Service Twenty-Four Hours a Day!

Being open twenty-four hours a day is one of the many services offered by L.L. Bean, Inc., a famous and remarkably successful sporting goods and clothing store in Freeport. The store was founded in 1905 by Leon Leonwood Bean. In 1912, Bean invented waterproof hunting boots, which he sold in mail-order catalogs. As the success of the store and the catalog grew, Bean added more sporting goods and a line of sturdy, comfortable clothes for the outdoor life — clothes that became very fashionable in the 1970s. The L.L. Bean retail store soon became the leading tourist attraction in Freeport. The store, which has a trout pond inside, even has its own zip code. The success of L.L. Bean and its products has helped promote Maine's image as a state filled with rugged individualists.

Electrical equipment, fourth in importance among manufactured goods, has gained prominence in part because of the most valuable electronic product — computer parts. Other goods made in Maine include leather products such as shoes, frozen-food products such as fish and potatoes, plastics, canned foods such as soups and chowders, and printed materials such as newspapers.

Transportation, Services, and Tourism

Maine has a good system of roads totaling about 23,000 miles (37,007 km). The state also supports a commuter line of railroads, as well as a railroad system that carries freight within the state. On the coast, ferries provide transportation routes between in-state ports and also between Maine and Nova Scotia, Canada. Several of Maine's ports can accommodate large ships. The busiest ports are Eastport, Portland, and Searsport. Eastport, which is the closest U. S. port to Europe, provides an entry point for oil that is shipped to Canada via pipeline. For ship repairs, the Bath Iron Works in Bath offers one of the nation's largest dry docks. Airports in Portland and Bangor have the most air traffic, including international flights.

Service industries, concentrated in metropolitan regions, make up the largest part of Maine's economy and provide the greatest number of jobs to its citizens. These jobs are found in the wholesale and retail trade of paper, pulp, and textiles, and in such retail businesses as car dealerships, discount stores, restaurants, and grocery markets. Service industry jobs are also found in community, business, and personal services, as well as in finance, insurance, and real estate. Government service jobs provide income for many Maine inhabitants. In addition, the tourist industry brings dollars to people who work in the state's local restaurants, shops, hotels, resorts, and pleasure cruise businesses.

▲ The Bath Iron Works, the oldest shipbuilding yard in the United States, is the largest private employer in Maine. Changes in methods and equipment help keep the facility state-of-the-art.

Made in Maine

Leading farm products and crops
Potatoes
Blueberries
Eggs
Milk

Other products
Paper and wood products
Transportation equipment
Electrical equipment
Leather products
Food products

Major Airports		
Airport	Location	Passengers per year (2000)
Portland International	Portland	13,790,115
Bangor International	Bangor	444,896

Voter Pride

> . . . no outside clamor, either of the press or of individuals, no prejudice or passion, no hope of benefit, or fear of injury to myself, no just indignation against the individual . . . no considerations of party, no regard for those I am most anxious to please, should induce me to swerve from the straight line of justice . . .
>
> — *William Pitt Fessenden, U.S. Senator, 1867*

Maine's citizens are proud of their system of government. Proof of this pride can be found in Mainers' involvement in their government — voter turnout in Maine often leads the nation.

The government of Maine is similar in structure to that of the United States federal government. Maine's government consists of three branches: the executive, the legislative, and the judicial. The executive branch, which includes the office of governor, ensures that the state's laws are carried out. The legislative branch, or state legislature, writes, amends, and repeals laws. The judicial branch, or court system, interprets the laws.

Maine's constitution was adopted in December 1819, three months before Maine became a state. Although it has been amended, or changed, more than 150 times since then, it still stands today. Any amendment to the constitution must be proposed by a two-thirds vote in the state legislature. To make the amendment into law, the state's voters must approve it by a majority (more than half). The constitution may also be amended by calling a constitutional convention, but the constitution has never been amended in this fashion.

The Executive Branch

The only executive official directly elected by Mainers is the governor. The state does not have a lieutenant governor, and the state legislature elects the other members of the

State Constitution

"**W**e the people of Maine, in order to establish justice, insure tranquility, provide for our mutual defense, promote our common welfare, and secure to ourselves and our posterity the blessings of liberty, acknowledging with grateful hearts the goodness of the Sovereign Ruler of the Universe in affording us an opportunity, so favorable to the design; and, imploring God's aid and direction in its accomplishment, do agree to form ourselves into a free and independent State, by the style and title of the State of Maine and do ordain and establish the following Constitution for the government of the same."

— *Preamble to the amended Maine State Constitution*

Elected Post in the Executive Branch		
Office	Length of Term	Term Limits
Governor	4 years	2 consecutive terms

executive branch — attorney general, secretary of state, state auditor, and state treasurer. The governor is limited to two consecutive four-year terms. He or she is empowered to enforce the laws of the state or to veto any bill that the legislature passes, in the event that it violates the constitution. The legislature may override a veto by a two-thirds vote.

The Legislative Branch

The state legislature is made up of two chambers — the senate and the house of representatives. Each of the 35 senatorial districts of Maine elect one senator, while the 151 representative districts each elect one representative. These 186 elected legislators make, amend, and repeal Maine's laws, as well as elect the people who will serve on the governor's cabinet of advisers. The legislators are elected to two-year terms. Until 1993, they could be reelected to an unlimited number of terms, but in that year a new law was passed that limited the number of consecutive legislative terms to four.

Both chambers of the legislature convene for two sessions a year in Augusta, the state capital. The impressive capitol building in which they convene was designed by Charles Bulfinch, a famous architect from Boston. The structure was built from 1829 to 1832, and much of it consists of Maine granite.

▼ Maine's capitol building houses the state senate and state house of representatives in separate wings. A statue representing wisdom sits atop the capitol dome and is plated with gold.

In 1910, in one of many renovations, the building's length was doubled by adding north and south wings. The house of representatives occupies the third and fourth floors of the north wing, while the senate has matching quarters in the south wing.

The Judicial Branch

Maine's judiciary includes its system of criminal and civil courts. The supreme judicial court, the state's highest court of appeals for all criminal and civil cases, meets in Augusta. A chief justice and six associate justices sit on the supreme court, each serving a seven-year term. The next highest court, the superior court, hears cases that require jury trials, as well as those cases appealed from lower courts. This court's sixteen justices also serve seven-year terms. In addition, the judiciary includes thirty-one district courts, which hear cases involving damages that are less than $20,000. The district courts are spread out over Maine's thirteen judicial districts, with judges who serve seven-year terms. The governor nominates all justices of the supreme, superior, and district courts, but they can only be appointed with approval of two-thirds of the senate.

Each county in Maine has a probate court. These courts are responsible for certifying that a will is authentic and that the terms of the will are carried out. They also deal with such matters as adoptions and legal guardianships. Unlike the appointed officials of higher courts, probate judges are elected by the people for terms of four years.

Local Government

Government in the United States is divided into federal, state, and local levels. The federal government's powers extend over the entire nation, while a state government has powers over state matters. Within a state, however, local governments operate county by county, town by town.

Legislature			
House	Number of Members	Length of Term	Term Limits
Senate	35 senators	2 years	4 consecutive terms
House of Representatives	151 representatives	2 years	4 consecutive terms

In Maine, local government follows a longstanding New England tradition. Towns, run by officials called selectmen, conduct regular town meetings where residents can speak for themselves on local matters. In this manner, citizens participate directly, making suggestions and voting on issues that affect them. Each of Maine's sixteen counties has its own government. The Native American population has three townships, each of which is self-governing.

Maine's cities have either a city-manager or a mayor-council form of government. Approximately 50 percent of Maine land is not part of a city or town. Much of this land belongs to lumber or pulp companies.

National Representation

Like every other state, Maine has two senators in the U.S. Senate. The number of Maine representatives in the U.S. House of Representatives, determined by the state's population, is just two. Each state selects "electors" to vote on the state's behalf in presidential elections. A state's Electoral College votes equal the total of that state's U.S. senators and representatives, so Maine has four Electoral College votes.

Maine Politics

Maine has long been a strongly Republican state. As early as the 1850s, when the Republican Party was established, Mainers leaned toward the party, which held an anti-slavery position. Later, business leaders in the state approved of the party's policies favoring big business. Some Democrats gained high offices in the early 1900s, but it was not until 1954, with the election of Democrat Edmund S. Muskie as governor, that the state's party politics became more balanced. Today, the two major parties share power with the Independent Party, which put the first Independent governor, Angus King, Jr., in the state capitol in 1994.

Kennebunkport: Presidential Retreat

The family of former U.S. President George Herbert Walker Bush has had a summer home in Kennebunkport since 1903. Bush, the forty-first president, was in office from 1989 to 1993. During that time, Kennebunkport became famous as the president's summer home and retreat. The tradition continued with President George W. Bush, son of George Herbert, elected in 2000. Residents of the area are proud of their famous summer visitors.

▶ Residents of Islesboro participate in small town politics. They attend a meeting at Town Hall to discuss local issues.

Seas, Trees, and More

> All I could see from where I stood
> Was three long mountains and a wood.
> — *"Renascence" by Edna St. Vincent Millay, 1912*

What you discover in Maine today depends on where you look. The natural world of islands, beaches, mountains, forests, and farms offers a long list of outdoor adventures. Historical sites and museums featuring history and maritime exhibits will take you on journeys into the state's rich past. In addition, art museums and galleries, concerts, and folk festivals provide a taste of the talent and culture in this fascinating state.

Visitors traveling north along the coast into Maine will come first to the city of Kittery. Several old mansions in the city reflect its past as a major shipbuilding center, including Lady Pepperell House, which dates from 1760. Many of Kittery's modern residents commute out of town for their jobs, but they shop close to home in the local retail outlets. Nearby York also has a long history. Its Old Gaol, a jail erected in 1719, is now a historical museum. Farther north, in Wells, the Rachel Carson National Wildlife Refuge honors the famous conservationist. The towns of Kennebunkport and Kennebunk are seaside resort communities with lovely old homes. In Kennebunkport, the Seashore Trolley Museum displays more than two hundred antique trolley cars. Kennebunk, meanwhile, is

▼ Hikers in Maine enjoy spectacular views along the Appalachian Trail, stretching from Maine to Georgia.

home to the famous Wedding Cake House, built in 1856 by a retired sea captain for his bride. Its elaborate wooden trim resembles the fancy frosting on a wedding cake.

Portland's many historical sites include Monument Square, in the city's downtown area, which dates back to the American Revolution. The city is also home to the state's most popular historic site, the Wadsworth-Longfellow House. Poet Henry Wadsworth Longfellow spent many summers in the house as a boy, and the house contains a treasure trove of his belongings and letters.

The Kennebec River, which flows to the coast from far inland, has many important towns and cities along its banks, including the state capital, Augusta. At Augusta's Old Fort Western, which dates back to the French and Indian War, guides wear colonial costumes and demonstrate how the colonists performed their everyday chores and crafts.

In Rockland, on the southwestern lip of Penobscot Bay, visitors can explore the Shore Village Museum, which contains a collection of lighthouse lenses. East of the bay, on Isle au Haut and, farther north, Mount Desert Island, is Acadia National Park, the only national park in New England. On Maine's border with Canada sits Saint Croix Island, home of the International Historic Site, which honors the historic beginning of Canada and the United States.

In the sparsely populated northern woods of Maine, at Moosehead Lake (shaped like the antlers and head of a moose), visitors can tour the Moosehead Marine Museum and take lake tours on a diesel-engine boat. In Auburn, in mid-August, the annual Great Falls Balloon Festival draws balloonists from around the country. Every August in the town of Presque Isle, the Northern Maine Fair provides its annual fun. This weeklong festival features food, square dancing, and games, as well as exhibits of prize livestock, potatoes, and pumpkins. In addition, local farmers compete in popular harness races.

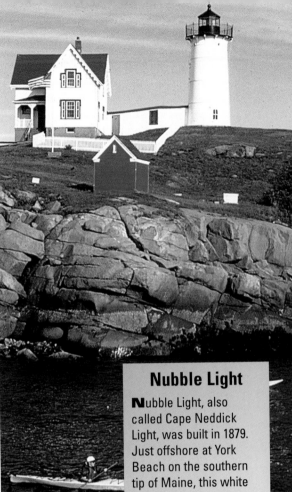

Nubble Light

Nubble Light, also called Cape Neddick Light, was built in 1879. Just offshore at York Beach on the southern tip of Maine, this white lighthouse overlooks the Atlantic Ocean, flashing a red light that serves as a navigational warning to passing ships. The facility was automated in 1987, at which time the last of its lightkeepers left. Today, Nubble Light, with its lightkeeper's house, oil house, storage building, and boathouse, is so picturesque that it is one of Maine's most frequently photographed lighthouses. The property is not open to the public and can only be reached by boat except in an unusually low tide, but roughly 250,000 visitors come each year to nearby Sohier Park just to view it.

Libraries and Museums

Maine's first library, founded in 1751, sent a traveling collection of books to parish houses in York and Kittery. Today, the state has about 275 public libraries, the largest of which are in Portland and Bangor. In Portland, the Maine Historical Society, founded in 1822, houses a large collection of books and manuscripts about the history of the state and New England. The Maine State Library in Augusta also contains a sizable collection of historical books.

Maine abounds with museums. In Augusta, the Maine State Museum features exhibits on the state's history, while Native American art and crafts are exhibited at the Abbe Museum in Bar Harbor, on Mount Desert Island. In Bath, the Maine Maritime Museum chronicles the importance of Maine's sailing and shipping history. The Portland Museum of Art offers paintings and sculptures for viewing, and numerous artists who have drawn their inspiration from Maine's notable natural beauty through the years now exhibit their work throughout the state. The museum at Bowdoin College in Brunswick is just one of many institutions and galleries that maintains a collection of

▲ T-shaped stocks stand outside the Old Goal, built about 1719. This former jail in Kittery is the oldest municipal building in the United States.

DID YOU KNOW?

The first blackboard was invented in Rumford in 1816. Schools have never been the same since! The first blackboards, as their name suggests, were made of black or dark gray slate. Later, "blackboards" were colored green, an easier background color for the eye to see the words written upon the board.

paintings by well-known artists who worked in Maine, including John Singer Sargent, Winslow Homer, and Andrew Wyeth.

Communications

There are seven daily newspapers published in Maine, the largest of which is the *Bangor Daily News*. In addition to dailies, Maine has about forty other newspapers. The state has a long history of news publishing that began with its first newspaper, the *Falmouth Gazette*, which first went to press in Falmouth (now Portland) in 1785. A variety of magazines have also originated in Maine, although many of them have readers throughout New England and beyond. These periodicals range in content from general interest to specialty subjects such as boating, fishing, hunting, antiques, horses, gardening, and technology. Perhaps the best known is *Down East* magazine.

In 1924, Bangor launched Maine's first radio station, WABI. Today Bangor continues to lead the way with not one, but six radio stations. In addition, the town claims the state's first TV station, WABI-TV, which began operating in 1953. About twenty-five television stations, ten of which are

▼ The L.L. Bean retail store in Freeport attracts crowds of tourists every year. L.L. Bean helped popularize Maine-style outdoor clothing and equipment.

cable, and many dozens of radio stations operate throughout the state.

Music and Theater

Portland lies at the center of cultural life in Maine. Aside from a famous symphony orchestra and many acclaimed theaters, the city has hosted noteworthy organ concerts since 1918 in its City Hall Auditorium. Bates College in Lewiston presents a nationally recognized dance festival each year, and the University of Maine in Orono hosts theater, dance, and musical events. In Monmouth, a lovely opera house called Cumston Hall makes concerts available to all by keeping ticket prices low. Bangor supports the Bangor Symphony, established in 1896.

The state also offers a number of summer music camps. Lakewood, near Skowhegan, is the home of the nation's oldest summer playhouse. Due to the success of this theater, other towns have been encouraged to open summer theaters of their own, such as ones located in Boothbay Harbor, Ogunquit, and Kennebunkport.

Sports

Maine supports no major league sports teams of its own, so many of the state's residents are fans of teams from Massachusetts. Mainers root for the Boston Red Sox in baseball, the Boston Celtics in basketball, and the New England Patriots in football. The state does have a very strong minor league hockey team, the Portland Pirates. The team often draws full-house crowds in Portland at the Cumberland County Civic Center.

Joan Benoit Samuelson, born in Cape Elizabeth in 1957, began running in high school after a skiing accident that resulted in a broken leg. In 1979, Samuelson, a Bowdoin

▲ Stephen King, probably Maine's best known contemporary writer, often chooses small Maine towns as settings for his mystery and horror novels.

DID YOU KNOW?

The movie director John Ford (1895–1973) was born in Cape Elizabeth. He won Academy Awards for four of his films: *The Informer, The Grapes of Wrath, How Green Was My Valley,* and *The Quiet Man.*

College graduate, became the first woman to win the Boston Marathon. She also won an Olympic gold medal in 1984 and the Sullivan Award as the nation's top amateur athlete in 1985.

Competitive sports aside, Maine offers plenty of outdoor recreation. Hearty souls hike the Appalachian Trail in Baxter State Park, climb Mount Katahdin, and camp and hunt in the state's forests. In winter, the mountains and forests of Maine offer trails for both downhill and cross-country skiers and snowshoers. In summer, both locals and visitors enjoy swimming, fishing, surfing, sailing, kayaking, and canoeing along the Atlantic coast and on Maine's rivers, streams, and lakes. Many spectators gather for the sailboat races at Boothbay Harbor's Windjammer Festival.

▼ WNBA guard Cindy Blodgett (right), of the Sacramento Monarchs, fends off guard Betty Lennox of the Minnesota Lynx. The Monarchs won the game 73–56.

Maine Greats

Ricky Craven, born in Newburgh, had his first full season as a National Association for Stock Car Auto Racing (NASCAR) racecar driver in 1989, in the Busch Grand National North Series. Craven earned the NASCAR Winston Cup Rookie of the Year in 1995, becoming the first driver to win the title in three key NASCAR touring events. Now living in Concord, North Carolina, Craven has gained national fame by competing in NASCAR's Winston Cup.

Cindy Lee Blodgett began her basketball career with her high school team, the Lawrence Bulldogs. Blodgett led the Bulldogs to four consecutive Class A state championships. Playing for the University of Maine's basketball team (1995–1998), the Black Bears, she was fourth on the NCAA all-time Division One scorers' list with 3,005 points. Blodgett was drafted into the Women's National Basketball Association (WNBA) in 1998.

Magnificent Mainers

Lives of great men all remind us
We can make our lives sublime,
And, departing, leave behind us
Footprints on the sands of time.

— *"A Psalm of Life"*
by Henry Wadsworth Longfellow, 1839

Following are only a few of the thousands of people who were born, died, or spent much of their lives in Maine and made extraordinary contributions to the state and the nation.

WILLIAM PEPPERELL
SOLDIER

BORN: *June 27, 1696, Kittery Point*
DIED: *July 6, 1759, Kittery*

Maine merchant Sir William Pepperell played a pivotal role in the struggle between the French and British in North America. In 1745, he led four thousand New England militiamen in the capture of the French fort of Louisbourg, Nova Scotia, a key stronghold for France. This victory for Maine and the British colonies is considered one of the most important turning points in the conflict, which culminated in the French and Indian War (1754–1763). When the war ended, all French claims to land in Maine were ended. Today, Lady Pepperell House, the stately home of the wife of William Pepperell, stills stands in Kittery, Maine.

JOHN RUSSWURM
JOURNALIST

BORN: *October 1, 1799, Port Antonio, Jamaica*
DIED: *June 17, 1851, Monrovia, Liberia*

In 1826, John Brown Russwurm became one of the nation's first African Americans to earn a college degree. Born of a slave woman and a planter from Virginia, he moved to New England as a child and, with help from his father and stepmother, attended school. He graduated from Bowdoin College in Brunswick, which, in 1802, had been one of the first colleges in the United States to open its doors to African Americans. In 1827, Russwurm helped establish *Freedom's Journal*, the country's first newspaper owned, operated, written, and edited by African Americans. He eventually lost his job with the newspaper because of his view that African Americans should return to Africa to create colonies. Russwurm emigrated to Liberia in 1829, and he eventually became governor of a colony at Cape Palmas.

DOROTHEA DIX
SOCIAL REFORMER

BORN: *April 4, 1802, Hampden*
DIED: *July 17, 1887, Trenton, NJ*

A tireless educator and social reformer, Dorothea Lynde Dix was a schoolteacher in Massachusetts by the time she was fourteen years old. She devoted herself to many causes, including the improvement of conditions in the country's jails, and during the Civil War she was the head of the Union army's nurses. Her efforts to educate people about the needs of mental patients was critical to the founding of hospitals for the mentally ill in several states.

HENRY WADSWORTH LONGFELLOW
POET

BORN: *February 27, 1807, Portland*
DIED: *March 24, 1882, Cambridge, MA*

Henry Wadsworth Longfellow spent his boyhood years in Maine. While at Bowdoin College, he decided to become a writer and drew upon Maine's beauty and history for inspiration and for the subject matter of many of his works. During the 1800s, Longfellow was the nation's best-loved poet. One of his works is "Evangeline" (1847), a long poem that tells the story of French Acadians who were deported from Canada as a result of land disputes between Britain and France. He also wrote "The Midnight Ride of Paul Revere" (1863) and "The Song of Hiawatha" (1855).

JAMES G. BLAINE
STATESMAN

BORN: *January 31, 1830, West Brownsville, PA*
DIED: *January 27, 1893, Washington, DC*

James Gillespie Blaine became a resident of Maine after he married Maine native Harriet Stanwood of Augusta in 1850. He became editor for the *Kennebec Journal* in 1854 and later assumed part ownership of the *Portland Advertiser*. His work in journalism was soon followed by a significant political career. Blaine first served in the Maine legislature. In 1863, he was elected to the U.S. House of Representatives, where he served as Speaker of the House between 1869 and 1875. He then served in the U.S. Senate, from 1876 to 1881. In 1881, Blaine became secretary of state under President James Garfield, but this post ended when Garfield was assassinated. Blaine ran unsuccessfully as the Republican candidate for president in 1884, and in 1889 he was again appointed secretary of state, under President Benjamin Harrison. In 1892, he finally returned to private life.

MILTON BRADLEY
ENTREPRENEUR

BORN: *November 8, 1836, Vienna*
DIED: *May 30, 1911, Springfield, MA*

Milton Bradley was an entrepreneurial genius. Born in Maine, Bradley grew up in Massachusetts, where he started a lithography shop in Springfield in 1860. Responding to a business slow-down, Bradley decided to create a new product that would make a profit but be easy to manufacture. He settled on printing board games in his shop and created a game called "The Checkered Game of Life." The game became very popular, selling more than 45,000 copies. In the aftermath of this success, Bradley formed Milton Bradley and Company to create more games. In 1880, the company began making jigsaw puzzles as well. Today, the company that bears Milton Bradley's name is the world's largest producer of games and puzzles.

HENRY GANNETT
GEOGRAPHER

BORN: *August 24, 1846, Bath*
DIED: *November 5, 1914, Washington, DC*

Henry Gannett was a graduate of Harvard University. In 1872, he joined the U.S. Geological and Geographical Survey of the Territories, acting as a topographer in the West. He became the chief geographer in charge of geographic mapping for the United States Geological Survey in 1882. Gannett spent the rest of his working life in that position, accomplishing such major tasks as organizing the work of the Census Bureau and helping to create the U.S. Board on Geographic Names in 1890. In 1888, Gannett also helped establish the National Geographic Society.

LOUIS SOCKALEXIS
ATHLETE

BORN: *October 24, 1871, Old Town*
DIED: *December 24, 1913, Burlington*

Louis Sockalexis was a Penobscot, born on a reservation in Old Town. From the time he was young, he showed a great talent for throwing, and he eventually had starring roles as a pitcher and an outfielder while he attended Holy Cross and then Notre Dame. From 1897 to 1899, Sockalexis played professional baseball for a team called the Cleveland Spiders, where he earned an awesome career batting average of .313. While playing, Sockalexis faced prejudice because of his Native American heritage. Opposing teams were known to greet him with imitation war whoops and war dances. Sockalexis's career ended early, due in part to an injury and in part to a problem with alcohol. His short career, however, helped open the way for other minority athletes who sought to use their talents in professional sports.

EDNA ST. VINCENT MILLAY
POET

BORN: *February 22, 1892, Rockland*
DIED: *October 19, 1950, Austerlitz, NY*

In 1923, Edna St. Vincent Millay became the first American woman to win the Pulitzer Prize for poetry. Her work speaks about young people and their feelings while growing up. She was just twenty years old when she saw her well-known poem "Renascence" published. In it, Millay used images of Maine coastal scenes to speak symbolically about a spiritual rebirth. Although she spent many years in Europe and New York, Millay often summered in Maine, spending time near Brunswick on Ragged Island.

STEPHEN KING
NOVELIST

BORN: *September 21, 1947, Portland*

Stephen King started writing stories at the age of seven. By the time he was twelve, he knew that stories of the weird and horrible were what he wanted to write. At age twenty, before graduating from the University of Maine with an English degree, King sold his first professional publication. After college, he married Tabitha Spruce and set himself on the road to a lifetime career of horror fiction. While writing his first novel, *Carrie*, he earned $1.60 per hour working in a laundry. With this novel's publication, however, and the movie that was subsequently made from it, King was well launched on a career that, to date, has produced dozens of successful works of fiction, including novels, screenplays, and short stories, and a work of nonfiction. Today, King is considered the most acclaimed and widely read of Maine's authors since Henry Wadsworth Longfellow, and he may well be one of the most commercially successful novelists of all time.

SAMANTHA SMITH
GOODWILL AMBASSADOR

BORN: *June 29, 1972, Auburn*
DIED: *August 25, 1985, Auburn*

Samantha Smith was only ten years old when she wrote a letter to Yuri Andropov, the newly appointed president of what was then the Soviet Union. At the time, there were many Cold War tensions between the United States and the Soviet Union. In her letter, written in 1982, Samantha pleaded for peace, saying, *I have been worrying about Russia and the United States getting into a nuclear war. Are you going to have a war or not? . . . God made the world for us to live together in peace and not fight.* In April 1983, long after Samantha's

letter was sent, she was called to the principal's office, where she learned that Andropov had been so impressed with her letter that he had published it in his official state newsletter. Soon after, a letter arrived from Androprov himself, inviting her to visit his country. Her visit, in 1983, made news around the world, and Samantha became a spokesperson for peace. Samantha and her father died in a plane crash two years later. After her death, the Soviet government issued a stamp in her honor. Mainers, proud of their young ambassador, have honored her memory with a life-size statue outside Augusta. She is shown releasing a dove, which is a symbol of peace, and beside her is a bear cub — a symbol of both the Soviet Union and her home state.

Maine

History At-A-Glance

8000 B.C.
Ancestors of Native Americans reach present-day Maine.

c. 1000
Vikings likely to have explored Maine coast.

1498
John Cabot explores Maine's coast, claiming the land for England.

1524
Giovanni da Verrazano explores coast of Maine, claiming land for France.

1604
French explorer Samuel de Champlain starts a colony near the St. Croix River.

1607
English settlers establish Popham Plantation colony near mouth of Kennebec River.

1629
Ferdinando Gorges takes control of Maine land grant.

1636
Maine's first government established.

1677
Maine becomes part of Massachusetts.

1775
Mainers capture the British ship *Margaretta* in Machias Bay in the first sea battle of the American Revolution.

1785
The *Falmouth Gazette*, Maine's first newspaper, is founded in what is today Portland.

1820
Maine becomes the twenty-third state on March 15, entering as a free state according to the Missouri Compromise.

1600   **1700**   **1800**

1492
Christopher Columbus comes to New World.

1607
Capt. John Smith and three ships land on Virginia coast and start first English settlement in New World — Jamestown.

1754–63
French and Indian War.

1773
Boston Tea Party.

1776
Declaration of Independence adopted July 4.

1777
Articles of Confederation adopted by Continental Congress.

1787
U.S. Constitution written.

1812–14
War of 1812.

United States

History At-A-Glance

1826
John Russwurm graduates from Bowdoin College in Brunswick, becoming one of the nation's first African-American college graduates.

1851
Maine is first state to outlaw the making and selling of alcohol.

1894
Maine completes the Aroostook Railroad, enabling the state's farmers to ship potato crops to other states.

1934
Maine ends prohibition.

1958
Edmund Muskie of Rumford is the first Democrat in the twentieth century elected by Mainers to the U.S. Senate.

1970
Maine joins the nation in celebrating the first Earth Day, inaugurating a decade of important environmental legislation in Maine.

1842
Webster-Ashburton Treaty settles border dispute between Maine and Canada, ending Aroostook War.

1860
Hannibal Hamlin of Paris Hill is elected vice president of the United States under President Abraham Lincoln.

1948
Margaret Chase Smith of Skowhegan wins one of Maine's seats in the U.S. Senate, becoming the first woman to serve in both houses of Congress.

1929
Banks, farms, and factories in Maine begin to fail as the Great Depression hits the nation.

1964
Maine supports a Democrat for president for the first time since 1912, voting for Lyndon B. Johnson.

1980
U.S. government pays $81.5 million to Penobscot, Maliseet, and Passamaquoddy for land seized unfairly.

1800	1900	2000

1848
Gold discovered in California draws eighty thousand prospectors in the 1849 Gold Rush.

1869
Transcontinental railroad completed.

1929
Stock market crash ushers in Great Depression.

1950–53
U.S. fights in the Korean War.

2000
George W. Bush wins the closest presidential election in history.

1861–65
Civil War.

1917–18
U.S. involvement in World War I.

1941–45
U.S. involvement in World War II.

1964–73
U.S. involvement in Vietnam War.

2001
A terrorist attack in which four hijacked airliners crash into New York City's World Trade Center, the Pentagon, and farmland in western Pennsylvania leaves thousands dead or injured.

▼ Lumberjacks cut trees while oxen haul them away in this woodcut of early Maine logging.

Festivals and Fun for All

Check web site for exact date and directions.

Acadian Festival, Madawaska

On Mount Desert Island in June each year, this festival focuses on the history and way of life of the Acadians, a group of Roman Catholic French Canadians who once lived in Maine.
www.townofmadawaska.com/cc.html

Blueberry Festival, Union

At the Blueberry Festival in August, visitors learn about the history of blueberries, how they grow, and their many delicious uses.
www.unionfair.org/Blueberry.cfm

Boothbay in Bloom, Boothbay Harbor

This botanical festival, which takes place in early June, brings together a display of fantastic flowers to celebrate the coming summer months. Merchants, local artisans, and other citizens present many colorful entries.
www.boothbayharbor.com/events_boothbayinbloom.asp

Clam Festival, Yarmouth

Folks gather in Yarmouth in July each year to sample the many delicious dishes made with clams. Prize-winning recipes and information about the clamming industry are available.
www.clamfestival.com

Fishermen's Festival, Boothbay Harbor

In April, people who fish in the region gather at this festival to compete in trap hauling. There is also a codfish relay, the Shrimp Princess Pageant, a lobster crate race, and an old-fashioned fish fry. Other foods can also be enjoyed during the festival at a pancake breakfast and a fish chowder contest.
www.boothbayharbor.com/events_fishermensfest.asp

Great Falls Balloon Festival, Auburn

Each August, balloonists from all over the country fill the skies above Auburn. The event offers food, entertainment, carnival rides, and balloon rides — fun for all ages.
www.greatfallsballoonfestival.com

Local Fairs, Bangor, Cumberland Center, Farmington, Fryeburg, Presque Isle, Skowhegan, Topsham, Union, and Windsor

Many towns host traditional fairs during summer and early autumn. Look for delicious local foods, livestock, agricultural displays, arts, crafts, and other attractions.
www.mainevacations.net/c1/fairs.htm

The Maine Festival,
Thomas Point Beach, Brunswick

This August festival features live music by folk, country, jazz, and rock performers from all over Maine. Visitors will also find local arts and crafts, workshops, giant puppets, and a variety of delicious foods.
www. mainearts.org/festival.html

Maine Lobster Festival,
Rockland

At the Maine Lobster Festival each summer, visitors learn about the history of this crustacean and sample the many delicious ways lobster can be eaten. Arts and crafts featuring this important state resource are also available.
www.mainelobsterfestival.com

Maine Potato Blossom Festival,
Rockland

This festival, held in July, is devoted to everything about the potato! Events include mashed-potato wrestling, a parade, a contest to choose the Maine Potato Queen, and many delicious potato recipes.
www.potatoblossom.org

National Folk Festival, **Bangor**

This festival, held in August, features special foods and crafts and a rich variety of music, including zydeco, blues, Gaelic, polka, Cajun, and bluegrass. Also included are folk dancing, special children's activities, and storytelling.
www.nationalfolkfestival.com

Northern Maine Fair,
Presque Isle

Held each year in the summer, this fair is the state's biggest. It runs for a week and is jam-packed with events and activities, including games, square dancing, puppet theater, a petting zoo, an antique car show, a demolition derby, and harness racing. Delicious foods are available, and there are also livestock and agricultural displays and competitions.
www.northernmainefair.com

Sugarloaf/Carrabassett Skiing Events, **Kingfield**

International skiing events take place from January through April at the Sugarloaf/Carrabassett resort area near Kingfield.
www.skicentral.com/events.html

Windjammer Days, **Boothbay Harbor**

Every year in June, Boothbay Harbor hosts a popular boat-racing regatta that draws sailboats from all over the country. Local restaurants offer seafood chowders and blueberry desserts, and a waterfront concert and harborside fireworks cap off the days' events.
www.boothbayharbor.com/events_windjammer.asp

▶ Schooners ply the waters in Boothbay Harbor, offering a reminder of the bygone era of sailing vessels.

Books

Dean, Julia. *A Year on Monhegan Island.* New York: Ticknor & Fields, 1995. Learn about the seasonal changes and the diverse plants and wildlife on this Maine island.

Doherty, Katherine M. and Craig A. Doherty. *The Penobscot.* Danbury, CT: Franklin Watts, 1996. An in-depth look at this group of Native Americans from Maine, with historical illustrations and photos.

Fazio, Wende. *Acadia National Park.* Danbury, CT: Children's Press, 1998. Take a trip through this beautiful national park, complete with maps and photos.

Kress, Stephen W. *Project Puffin: How We Brought Puffins Back to Egg Rock.* Gardiner, ME: Tilbury House, 1999. This book is a first-person account of Project Puffin, an effort to restore a colony of puffins to an island off Maine's coast. Containing beautiful photographs, the book offers an excellent introduction to both the puffins and the protection of wildlife habitats in Maine.

Marsh, Carole. *Maine "Jography": A Fun Run Thru Our State!* Bath, NC: Gallopade Publishing Group, 1990. This adventure takes you on an imaginary "run" to the many sights throughout the state of Maine.

Wilmerding, John. *The Artist's Mount Desert: American Painters on the Maine Coast.* Princeton, NJ: Princeton University Press, 1994. Read about and look at the work of painters who were inspired by the rugged Maine landscape.

Web Sites

▶ Official state web site
www.state.me.us

▶ Maine State Symbols
www.50states.com/maine.htm

▶ Maine Historical Society
www.mainehistory.org

▶ Acadia National Park
www.nps.gov/acad

Note: Page numbers in *italics* refer to maps, illustrations, or photographs.